W9-CLI-842

Keep Yourself Safe

Being Safe with People

Honor Head

W

FRANKLIN WATTS
LONDON · SYDNEY

Franklin Watts
First published in Great Britain in 2015 by The Watts Publishing Group

Picture Credits: Cover © Dreamstime; 1, 4, 5, 6, 8, 9, 11, 12, 14, 15, 16, 17, 18 bottom, 19, 20 © Dollar Photo Club; 7, 10, 13 © iStock; 18 top © Shutterstock

Series Editor: Eloise Macgregor
Series Designer: Alix Wood
Illustrations: Alix Wood
Consultant: Dianne Lewis, The Lewis Bateson Centre for Personal and
    Family Development

Dewey number 613.6
HB ISBN 978 1 4451 4429 0

Printed in China

Franklin Watts
An imprint of
Hachette Children's Group
Part of The Watts Publishing Group
Carmelite House
50 Victoria Embankment
London EC4Y 0DZ

An Hachette UK Company
www.hachette.co.uk

www.franklinwatts.co.uk

FSC
www.fsc.org

MIX
Paper from
responsible sources
FSC® C104740

Contents

Feeling safe......................................4

Good friends 6

Bullying 8

Stay safe from bullies..................10

Stay safe online...........................12

Stranger safety...........................14

Your close family..........................16

Keeping secrets...........................18

Keep safe quiz 20

Glossary.......................................22

Further information...................24

Index..24

Hi!
I'm Safety Sam.
I'll help you learn
how to be safer
with people.

Feeling safe

Most of the people you know, such as your family and friends, will be kind and helpful. It's important that you feel safe with the people around you.

But sometimes things go wrong. You should not feel scared by grown ups or other children. If you want to talk about something that is upsetting you or making you feel scared or angry, speak to a trusted adult.

Ask Safety Sam

Who is a trusted adult?

- A grown up you feel safe with. It might be your mum or dad or **carer**, a grandparent or another family member.

- It could be a special teacher at school or your favourite librarian.

- It could be your best friend's mum or someone who runs your club.

Good friends

Friends are special. You can share all sorts of things with friends and have lots of fun together.

You must not feel you have to do something because all your friends say you should. This is called **peer pressure**. It can be hard to say 'no' when everyone else says yes.

BEWARE

This boy is doing something dangerous and silly. If a friend asks to you to do something like this, you can say no. If the person is a good friend, they will understand.

Ask Safety Sam

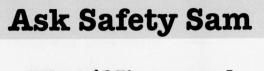

What if I'm scared and don't want to do what my friends say?

- Sometimes being scared is a good thing. Being scared can stop you doing dangerous things and keep you safe.

- If it's hard to say no, tell your friends someone is expecting you at home and leave.

- If your friends try to make you do things you don't want to, look for new friends. Try a new club or group.

Bullying

Bullying is when other people do nasty things like pinching, pushing, hitting or name calling over and over again.

Being made to feel stupid or being ignored is also bullying.

If you are being bullied you should not feel embarrassed or ashamed. It's not your fault. Talk to a trusted adult about it or phone a **helpline**. They can help you make the bullying stop.

Bullying can happen anywhere. People can be bullied by other kids at school and at home by brothers and sisters or other family members.

Ask Safety Sam

Why do some people become bullies?

- People turn into bullies for all sorts of reasons. It could be because they are being bullied themselves.

- Perhaps they are trying to look good in front of their friends.

- Maybe they are jealous of the person they are bullying.

Stay safe from bullies

Most bullies are **cowards** and pick on people smaller or younger than themselves. You must keep yourself safe from bullies.

Try not to be alone with the bully at any time. Leave the room or walk away when the bullying starts. If you can, take a deep breath, look at the bully and say 'Stop it now' in a firm voice.

In the playground stick with friends or stay close to where there is a teacher or adult supervisor.

BEWARE

Always report
bullying, whether it's
at home, at school or
on the street. Tell a
trusted adult or phone
a helpline.

Ask Safety Sam

What if the bullies follow me home?

• Tell an adult. If the bullies are from your school, the school should do something about it.

• Walk home through busy streets and avoid parks and quiet lanes.

• If you can, ask an adult to meet you or give you a lift in a car, or walk home with friends.

Stay safe online

Being online is fun and a great way to keep in touch with friends and family but it's important to stay safe online.

Get a smart **password**. This should be a mix of letters and numbers but not your birthday. Never tell anyone your password or write it down where anyone else could find it.

Never give out **personal details** to people online. Be careful sharing photos or videos – you don't know who may see them.

Don't meet up with anyone you've only met online. If you can't see someone, you don't know if they really are who they say they are.

Ask Safety Sam

How can I stop being cyberbullied?

• Cyberbullying is when people are nasty to you on your mobile phone, computer or tablet. If you are being cyberbullied, tell a trusted adult or phone a helpline.

• Don't answer nasty messages, texts or posts. Show them to an adult.

• Most cyberbullies will get bored if you don't answer their nasty messages.

Stranger safety

Most **strangers** are friendly and will be pleased to help if you are in trouble, but always be careful with strangers.

If a stranger talks to you, be polite and move away. Don't give them your personal details. NEVER get into a car with a stranger, even if the stranger knows your name and you see them every day, maybe on the way to school.

Ask Safety Sam

Who should I ask for help if I am out alone and can't talk to strangers?

- Look for a **safe person** such as a **traffic warden**, police officer or **lollipop person**.

- Look for a hospital, bank, post office or library and speak to someone who works there.

- Always have enough money so you can phone home from a public phone box or keep a mobile phone for emergencies.

BEWARE

Don't get close to strangers especially if they are in a car. If a stranger tries to grab you, scream and shout 'Stop' or 'No' and run to a place where there are shops and other people.

Your close family

Your close family are people you live with such as brothers and sisters, parents, carers, aunts and uncles or grandparents.

Even though you live with your family you should be allowed to be private when you do things like dressing and undressing and using the bathroom.

BEWARE

No one in your family should hurt you, call you names, bully you or frighten you. If they are, you must tell someone.

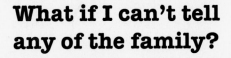

Ask Safety Sam

What if I can't tell any of the family?

- Phone a helpline. Check out helplines online and at the back of this book.

- Tell a teacher or another trusted adult.

- If you know where the police station is, go there and ask to speak to a police officer.

Keeping secrets

A big hug and a friendly kiss with someone you love and trust is special, but your family and friends should not make you feel scared or embarrassed.

No-one has the right to make you do things that you think are wrong. It is hard to say 'no' to people you love, but if they are making you feel bad, you must tell.

BEWARE

You should never keep a secret because you are scared. If someone asks you to keep a bad secret, tell a trusted adult, such as a nurse or teacher, or phone a helpline.

Ask Safety Sam

What is the PANTS rule?

• The PANTS rule helps you to remember that everything under your pants or swimming costume are your private parts and no one should ask to see or touch them.

P Privates are private

A Always remember your body belongs to you

N No means no

T Talk about secrets that upset you

S Speak up, someone can help

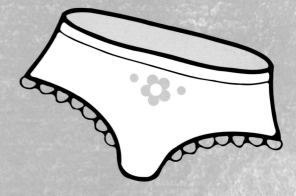

Keep safe quiz

Answer the questions to find out how you can stay safe with people.

1. Who is a trusted adult?
   a. Someone you see every day
   b. A grown up who makes you feel safe and who you trust
   c. Your neighbours

2. When is it good to say "no"?
   a. When someone asks you to help with the housework
   b. When your teacher tells you to behave
   c. When your friends ask you to do something dangerous?

3. What should you never do online?
   a. Talk to your friends
   b. Give strangers your personal details
   c. Try new websites

4. Which one of these is a PANTS rule?
   a. Privates are private
   b. Never have a hug
   c. Stay in your room all the time

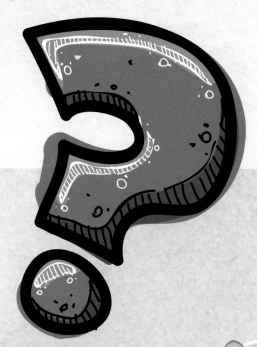

Safety Sam Says

Who would you ask for help if you were out with a friend and felt scared?

Why would you ask that person?

Glossary

carer The person who looks after you at home.

cowards People who are too scared to do the right thing.

cyberbullying When someone is made to feel sad or scared by threats and messages on their mobile, computer or other digital tablet.

helpline A telephone number that you can call to speak privately to someone who will listen to your problems and try to help you.

lollipop person A person who helps children to cross the road safely, especially near a school.

peer pressure Peers are people who are the same age as you. Peer pressure is when you think you have to do what they all do so that they stay your friends and don't laugh at you or tease you.

personal details Facts about you that can help someone find out who you are, such as your name, address, school or club you go to, or where you go to play.

safe person Someone you feel safe with and trust.

smart password A password that is difficult to guess. It should not be your name, your pet's name, or your birth date. It should contain letters and numbers.

strangers Anyone you don't know, men and women, old people and young people.

traffic warden A person whose job it is to make sure cars and other vehicles are parked properly.

Answers from page 20-21
1) b 2) c 3) b 4) a

Further Information

Books

Thomas, Pat, *I Can Be Safe*, Wayland, 2014

Barraclough, Sue, *Your Own Safety* (Stay Safe), Heinemann Library, 2008

Website

Topics about keeping yourself safe from hazards.
http://www.cyh.com/HealthTopics/
HealthTopicCategories.aspx?&p=288

Every effort has been made by the publisher to ensure that this website contains no inappropriate or offensive material. However, because of the nature of the Internet, it is impossible to guarantee that the content of this site will not be altered. We strongly advise that Internet access is supervised by a responsible adult.

Index

bullying 8, 9, 10, 11, 13, 17

carers 5, 16

cyberbullying 13

family 4, 5, 9, 12, 16, 17, 18

friends 4, 6, 7, 9, 10, 11, 12, 18

helplines 8, 11, 13, 17, 18

keeping secrets 18

online safety 12, 13

PANTS rule 19

passwords 12

peer pressure 6

police officers 15, 17

saying 'no' 6, 7, 15, 18, 19

strangers 14, 15

teachers 5, 10, 17

trusted adults 4, 5, 11, 13, 17, 18